Paranormal Poetry

A CHAPBOOK OF POEMS BY GHOSTS
OF THE SOUTH CAROLINA LOWCOUNTRY

DON FOXE

CABALLUS
PRESS™

Copyright © 2 0 1 8 donfoxe

Written by Don Foxe. donfoxe.com

Produced by Caballus Press, USA Division
www.caballuspress.com

Stock images are used for illustrative purposes only.
Stock imagery from Pixabay.com, Unsplach.com and Stock-dobe.com modified for use in this book.
Photograph attributions with images. Creative Commons Licensing guidelines followed.

ISBN: 978-1-7321036-1-0

Acknowledgments

Author's back cover photograph courtesy of *Abri Kruger Photography*, South Africa.

Cover graphics, original and modified interior artwork by Don Foxe. Photographs used and/or modified to produce graphic art by Ellen Pearson.

My love and appreciation to Sarah for continuing to support my late-night hours squirreled away in my office.

The following sites provided valuable information for my research for this chapbook.

https://www.talesofthelowcountry.com

http://www.hauntedplaces.org/beaufort-sc

http://ghostsnghouls.com/tag/haunted-beaufort

http://www.beaufortonline.com

https://www.sciway.net/hist/indians

http://www.u-s-history.com/pages/h637.html

http://www.bluffton.com/historic-haunted-bluffton

http://beaufortcountyhistoricalsociety.org

Poem 1

The Dwarf, The Castle, and the Chanson.

I suppose the sight of an older man with a guitar is not particularly odd. That I sat by a creek on damp scrub grass could be considered bucolic. The evening, having rolled beyond midnight, would make the scene difficult to explain. Luckily, no Sheriff's Deputy arrived to escort me off the private property.

Fingering the light melody of the chanson, keeping the music low, I watched the mist play across the still water. A common flow-through not five-feet across nor ten-inches deep. The type of creek you can watch grow and become a gushing rapid with rain. By my vision, limited by lack of light, it looked like a long, thin, shallow pool.

The full moon provided the only illumination; amber-yellow and broken by oaks and pines. Enough for me see the mist. Enough someone in the 1850s Italian-style house, set on the gentle swell above and behind, could see me. Should they stand at a second-story window at the back of the manse longer than a fleeting moment.

Claudin de Sermisy composed one-hundred-seventy-five chansons in his life. His music famous in mid-Sixteenth-Century France. The light, graceful songs never written for guitar, but hauling a harpsichord around seemed more work than the potential reward. Plus I don't play the harpsichord.

Or violin, or viola, or anything the composer had in mind in the 1560s.

I could have used my electronic keyboard. The electrical extension cord might have been suspicious.

The acoustic guitar would do. Most of the notes were repeated and played quickly. It gave the music a dance-like quality. The type of music and within the proper time-frame to attract the attention of a French jester who lived and died in the Sixteenth Century.

To improve my chances of attracting the dwarf, I chose a song with the topic of a beautiful young woman forced to marry an ugly, unvirile older man. I had been surprised to learn many of the chansons written during the Renaissance used similar themes.

Okay. Live with it. You snare ghosts your way. I'll use mine. For your information, I have used music to entice spirits to manifest since I discovered the method, accidentally, as a young boy stuck in Paris. Younger, by far, than others in my grade-level at the British International School. Often left on my own by a father busy with high-level foreign affairs of state - also known as cocktail parties. I taught myself how to play on a used-guitar bought at a flea market in the Latin Quarter. The strings worn shiny where the previous owner fingered notes and strummed without the aid of a pick.

I would sit on the roof of the apartment building, the lights of the City of Lights spread across my world, and force my finger tips to hold down the thin wires as my thumb slid across them to produce sounds.

Eventually sounds became melodies. One melody stuck in my head. A simple tune I repeated on the second-hand guitar. My back against a mechanical shack, knees up, and the too-large-for-me guitar propped in my lap, I watched smoke curl and begin to weave around the forest of antennas and wires. It seemed to dance to the song. I stopped playing. The smoke ceased moving, despite the warm breeze crossing the rooftop. I felt the request. I strummed the simple melody, the smoke danced, and my first contact with a ghost lasted thirty-minutes.

Fifty-years later I sit beside a shallow creek in the middle of Beaufort, South Carolina attempting to make contact with a French Huguenot dwarf, former jester, and current reoccurring spirit. A man who died in 1562 at Charlesfort, miles distant from this place.

I transferred the minim-crotchet-crotchet notations on the music sheets into a shorter version I could remember. The combination of notes, repeated more often, became a mesmerizing rhythm. The pattern reminded me of lyric poetry, quickly lulling me to ease. Luring Gauche to the grassy bank.

The mist crossed onto the land. A short, thick man with brooding eyes stood before me. His wide forehead topped by a slouchy beret. He wore a rough shirt, leather britches, and no shoes. His arms hung short, his small hands open. A scraggily beard with silver beads woven in beneath his chin.

I expected a jester's outfit and hands dripping in blood. I got a miniature pirate.

"Music from my past," he said. "What do you want?"

Histories of South Carolina's Lowcountry contain stories of hauntings. Enough spirits to support a thriving business in tours of haunted locations. Ghost excursions exist from Charleston, SC to Savannah, Georgia. Books and articles detailing the hundreds of ghosts, spirits, and specters linked to the region are available by the barrel.

I love history, enjoy reading, and maintain a passion for ghosts. For decades I set aside my musical connection to those gone-but-still-here to pursue the more mundane aspects of the living. Achieving success included moving to the southeastern corner of South Carolina, opening a fitness center on Hilton Head Island, and purchasing a home in Bluffton, across the bridge from the island.

Local phantoms perked my interest. With fewer years left ahead of me, and no longer concerned what people might think of my rediscovered hobby, I decided to investigate a few of these stories.

Did I know music would still create a connection? Nope. I decided the best test case would be the ghost of a French dwarf reported to haunt the Joseph Johnson house in Beaufort, SC. The mind-Eighteen-Hundred's structure of grand Italian-design known locally as The Castle.

Gauche was said to have been a jester by trade, a Huguenot in belief, and a member of the group brought to the area in 1562 by Jean Ribaut to escape persecution in Europe. They establish Charlesfort on what is currently Parris Island. If Gauche really worked as a jester in the time of Charles IX, the chanson should catch his ear.

"A poem," I replied.

A point I should make before you doubt (more) my story. Ghosts do not talk in their native language. In my experience, they do not talk at all. Communications are telepathic in nature. Even if sounds are made, the living hear in their own language. I am sure, with the abundance of non-living entities flitting about, there are exceptions. For me, english is my predominant language. English is what I hear when a spirit communicates.

"A poem?" Specters are more comfortable with startling people than being startled. My request not one the dead man expected. "Why would I create a poem? Why would you ask for one?"

"As a jester, I thought it would be an appropriate method for you to pass along anything you might wish to say," I answered. "A poem will be something people will remember."

The dwarf stared. Not a comfortable place to be, sitting on damp grass while a ghost tried to decide the level of my sanity. He did not simply return to mist and evaporate; which I took as a good sign. Afraid he might still do just that, I kept talking.

"No one knows why you appear at this house," I said. "It's miles away from Charlesfort and built three-hundred-years after your death. No one knows why you leave red hand-prints on the windows, or even exactly how you died. I've heard disease, hanging, and murdered."

"I was murdered," he said. "Hanged by the good French protestants Ribaut left behind. Fellow Huguenots escaping death from people who thought us different and dangerous. Can you imagine someone thinking me different or dangerous?"

Gauche's face did not change, but laughter filled the space within my head. Not happy laughter, but the laughter used when crying is not sad enough to express an emotional pain.

"I was treated as an outcast by outcasts from the moment I boarded till the final kick of my boots. Twice cursed. My choice of religion and God's choice to make me a dwarf."

I began a soft strumming of the chanson, allowing my fingers to work as I kept my attention on the ghost. I wanted the music to draw forth the man's pain. Let emptiness from my silence pull his thoughts to fill the void.

"Five of us left the island to look for wild game, berries, or anything we could take back to eat," he said. "I found a bunch of wild blackberries a few yards from where you sit. My sack almost filled, I heard a cry. A cry of a person, quickly muffled. I left my berries, pulled my knife, and hurried to this place. One of the fine pious men of our new colony was trying to force his cock into a young native girl. We knew natives lived near us, but none had attempted to make contact. Nor had any attempted us any harm."

I slowed the rhythm of the song.

"I am a little person, but I am strong. I pulled him off the girl, and lifted her from the dirt. In fact, she stood almost exactly where you now sit," he said. "When I turned, the bastard tried to stab me with his knife. We fought. I won."

This was different. I had listened to ghosts before. Held conversations with some. The norm was they lament something. I listen; they finish their tale and leave. As the dwarf spoke his simple narrative, I saw the action. Not playing out before me, but as if my imagination suddenly included three-dimensional depth. I could feel his anger, her fear, and the rapist's lust turned to hatred.

"When the others came at my call and found the bastard dead, they tied my hands. I was pushed back to the settlement. They buried the man I killed, called a jury, listened to my story and convicted me of murdering a fellow Huguenot over the questionable virtue of a savage. For saving the child, my reward was a breathtaking view of the Sound from a cross-arm."

"You return to this spot because this is where you saved the native girl," I said.

"My single greatest moment of honor," he said. "The blood on my hands is my own. I brought it upon myself. *Do onto others.*"

"Leaving handprints on the windows?" I asked.

"A jester's calling card," he said. "Gauche was here. Tell your friends."

The spirit wavered. I thought he would disappear. Instead, he came a step closer, his appearance more defined.

"I hope your memory is as well-tuned as your instrument. Here is your poem."

It only took my lifetime,
    and my life, to understand
You need not height to stand tall -
    to be counted as a man.

Juggle, tumble. Sing a song;
    I entertained the crowded halls.
They laughed and clapped for the clown,
But for the dwarf - silence falls.

I sailed not for adventure,
    but for faith and fealty.
Raised my hand for every task
On the land or when at sea.

Faith in Father, Son, and Ghost -
Hoped my brethren would see
    me as an equal in their eyes.
Not just the dwarf I'm forced to be.

According to the pious -
    all those God-forsaken men -
I murdered a man by choice.
My choice to save a heathen.

No Charlesfort laws were broken,
    except by me for living.
Hatred, bias, bigotry
    leave no space for forgiving.

It only took my lifetime,
    and my life, to understand
The laws that men believe in
Are as solid as the sand.

I haunt the place I stood tall.
A reminder to this land
Of the right choice made one night
By Gauche - not the dwarf - the man.

Tales of Beaufort, Nell S. Graydon
is a fine book to read more about the Castle. Visit any Lowcountry website regarding haunted places, tours, etc.

You can search chansons and/or Claudin de Sermisy for more on French Renaissance music.

The Castle is on Craven Street in Beaufort, SC.

You can also search for Beaufort, SC Tours, haunted and otherwise.

Joseph Johnson House in Beaufort, SC.
https://www.flickr.com/photos/anoldent/

Poem 2

An Unexpected Encounter

Hilton Head Island provides a home for several ghosts and poltergeists. The most famous being The Blue Lady. The young woman died following the hurricane of 1898. Story goes her father, the lighthouse keeper, had a heart attack while tending the light during the storm. He made her promise to keep it lit before his final breath.

Heroically she maintained the light, but the combination of exposure and exhaustion resulted in her own death a few weeks later.

Originally, her ghost was seen in the area of Palmetto Dunes, the location of the lighthouse. In 1966, Charles E. Fraser relocated the lighthouse and the keepers' cottages to the southern part of the island; Harbour Town in Sea Pines Plantation.

The Blue Lady apparently relocated with her home and became enamored with CQ's, the restaurant located next to the repositioned cottages. The restaurant is said to experience her presence with unexplained bottle shaking, furniture rearranging, and water faucets turned on when no one is present.

These poltergeist-like activities seemed far different from the first sightings of the blue specter around the original location for the buildings in Palmetto Dunes. Then she appeared as a young woman dressed in blue, or accompanied by a blue glow.

The changes in locations, and the curious changes in activities made the Blue Lady my next target. What music would a twenty-one-year-old woman listen to in the late Nineteenth Century? The available options almost overwhelmed the project. From Ragtime to Sousa marches. I could use Irish melodies or ditties from Broadway plays. This is, and was then, the South. Hymns and spiritual music were both popular, and not only on Sundays.

The best thing about this next adventure was the location. Sitting on a rocking chair, beneath moss-covered oaks, with a beer and mosquito repellant is a much better gig than trespassing on wet grass.

The beer safely hidden within a foam cup, with lid and straw for disguise, I sat back and strummed "My Wild Irish Rose." Though it was past midnight, the bars and restaurants, as well as the boats and homes hosting late-night parties, made my presence un-noteworthy to the security guards who roamed the island's most famous area.

CQ's and the cottages are a block or so from the actual harbor. My rocking chair sat beneath an ancient oak where I could see the restaurant, smell the Harbour Town Bakery, and not drawn attention myself.

I moved from Irish-based tunes to hymns. An hour in, my beer gone and my butt beginning to complain about the wooden slats, I contemplated a rousing John Phillip Sousa march. A difficult thing to do with an acoustic guitar.

"If you're doing this for the Blue Lady, you're wasting your time."

The voice, so near I heard every word perfectly, startled me. The image of the person now sitting in the rocking chair, empty all evening until now, dropped my jaw. I immediately wondered if my beer order included something special.

"I thought she haunted the cottages," I said in an attempt to carry on a conversation while trying to recover some composure.

"Nah. She's still up where they used to sit."

The apparition was dressed in deerskin. A v-neck pullover top with short, wide sleeves. The light, now that bars and restaurants had closed, came from antique looking street-lamps, the little ground lights used to show the brick pathway, and whatever illumination left on inside businesses that leaked through windows. I think his arms were tattooed, but it could have been paint. Long pants of the same deerskin covered his lower body. When he crossed his leg, I saw a sandal of some type of hide.

"People say her ghost wanders around that restaurant (I indicated CQs')."

"People say many stupid things," he replied, rocking the chair with the one foot still on the ground. "I rattle bottles and mess with the electricity. Sometimes, if someone is really a pain, I untie their boat."

"I've heard of no story about a Native American spirit on the island. No one has ever seen you?"

"Children, sometimes," he answered. As my eyes became accustomed to the light and my heart recovered from his arrival, I made out a few more details. His head was shaven on both sides with the black hair in the middle cut low. His nose was wide, more African than native American, though his lips were not as pronounced. He wore a leather lanyard around his neck. The end disappeared beneath his tunic.

"Dogs see me," he added. "Was a time, back when whites began building on top of the burial mounds, I tried scaring them off by hootin' and cursin' at them. Didn't stop them from building. I've been mostly watching since then. Making some mischief now and then for entertainment. Learning."

"Learning?"

"I was my tribe's medicine man. Learning was important when I lived. Well, not so much my final years. After I been dead a while, I realized I could still learn. Learned a lot since they brought in the lighthouse and the settlement grew from the sound to the ocean. More people are within earshot of where we sit now than lived in my time. I could have walked for a month when I still lived, and I would have run into fewer people than if you walk from here to the other side of the harbour."

"If you've stayed away from being seen for so long, why are you with me tonight?"

"Liked the music. Recognized what you were up to. Thought maybe it was a sign for me to pass along my story."

"I'd love to hear it," I said. Curiosity has such a fine way of displacing anxiety. Both reactions feel the same, but one pulls you closer while the other makes you shy away.

My name is Stands-By-Oak. I was the medicine man and spiritual guide for my tribe. Part of the Yamassee. My father told me tales from his father's people going back to the first tribe. Once our people lived among the jungles in a land hot all year. We lived in villages so large you could take a day to walk from one side to the other. Temples rose to the sky. Stone buildings protected us, unlike the log huts and palmetto thatch roofs of my own tribe.

God became angry. My ancestors were fierce, and spent many days warring against any other tribe discovered near their lands. God tired of my ancestors trying to become gods, so he stopped the rains. After many years, crops died. Animals died. People died.

The medicine men gathered the great tribe and divided it into smaller tribes. Each group moved away from the stone city. Other cities were also abandoned. People joined the small clan groups, or made their own.

The tribe of my father's fathers travelled north. Some clans stopped and settled new areas. Some continued to look for a place more like the first home. Deserts, mountains, and swamps became temporary places. The final clan left reached the great ocean. The same ocean that bordered our first home. The sea the sun rose from each morning.

Forests were dense and game plentiful. Soil was rich for growing. The local tribes did not like us, but they did not attack us. There were rivers and lands enough for everyone.

By the time my father died, and I became the spirit guide, my people lived on the bluffs of a wide river that flowed to and from the great ocean. Fish, and deer, and bears, and small animals plentiful. When the year was hot and the air damp and heavy, the winds along the bluff kept us cooled. When planting ended and the air grew cold, we would use rafts and canoes to cross the sound and set up our winter village on the southern end of the largest wooded island. Winds from the great ocean waters kept the island warmer than the mainland. The dense forest provided shelter and food.

During one of the times we camped on the island, the Coosa destroyed our huts along the bluff. We returned to ashes. Our Chief held great hatred against the Coosa for this. We rebuilt our huts. That winter, after we moved to the island, the Chief decided we would visit the Coosa and teach them not to mess with the Yamassee.

I set protections around our village. I called on the oldest spirits, the ones who built the shell rings we discovered many years before, to extend their protection from the circle to my people. I placed my own family inside the tribe's community hut, a large round building of the heaviest logs placed in the center of our winter village. I gave my wife and my three sons necklaces, each with a claw from a bear I had killed when I was a boy. I spread salt taken from the ocean around the entire village.

The Chief and every able man, including me, took our canoes and sang as we rowed to the shore of the mainland. Painted for war, we ran the trails our tribe knew from living in this land for generations. We reached the Coosa village when the night was dark, clouds covered the stars, and Mother Moon set low beyond our enemy's huts.

Our attack was loud and fierce as the stories of our ancestors. Spears, axes, and knives slashed as they lead us through doorways. Women and children were drug from their sleep, pressed together with old men in the center of their village. Some of our bucks took Coosa women into the dark woods.

I noticed the failure of the Coosa braves to repel our raid. I hurried to my Chief, crying only women and young ones were here. Where were the warriors?

By the time we returned to our village on the island, the Coosa had come and gone. Everyone left behind was dead. My family dead. All of my spells worthless. The protections could not stop the weapons of the Coosa. Unlike the Yamassee, who left the women and children alive when we raced away, the Coosa left no one. They did not even take slaves.

We built a dozen mounds to cover our dead. The Chief called the warriors together, and they left to avenge our tribe. I could not go. I would not go. I considered it my fault my family, all the families, died unprotected.

I lived the rest on my life alone. Others who lived on the island, and those who would come to this place while I lived knew of my existence. I left them alone. They left me to my sorrows.

When I died, no one placed my body in a mound. Animals and birds took me. Foxes and raccoons scattered my bones. I am a part of this land.

I cannot tell you what became of the men of the Yamassee. I no longer feel the presence of Yamassee. Not just those left of my tribe, but of any of the tribes.

My spirit walked uneasy. My soul cried in anger. After so many seasons of pain, I began to ease. I no longer care if people crossed over the graves of my family. It does not matter no one remembers the tribe that lived here. I have learned to accept my guilt.

"You want me to pass along your story?" I asked.

"The story of my life is not important," Stand-By-Oaks answered. "I thought if I told someone, it might free my spirit from this place. I'm still sitting here, so I guess not."

"I was going to ask the Blue Lady for a poem," I said. "A chance for her to tell her story in a way others would always remember. Would you like to try that?"

"Poem?" The ghost of the Yamassee spirit wavered. Gauche did the same thing before he gave me his poem. I believe spirits live in many times at once. I also think this out-of-focus event is a moment when a ghost phases between times.

"Not a poem," Stands-By-Oak said, his form more solid for an ethereal being. "No one ever heard my death song. Would that do?"

"I'd be honored."

Mother Night clouds my eyes.
My family waits at the shore
    with a long canoe and a space for me.
Follow my fathers to hunt forever.

Remember the bear my arrow took
    before my twelfth winter.
Remember the sea eagle that watched over me.
Remember the many fires and song of life shared.
Remember the battles and see my scars of victory.

Watch over these woods that shelter me
And watch for the storms that strike fire.
Tend the young, hunt the old, and face the mighty
One-to-one as I did.
    As my father did.
      As my brothers did.
Remember me as brave.

Forgive me my children,
Left circled by magic too weak to save them.

Forgive me my wife,
Gone long before my heart could forget
    or forgive.

Death walks as a brother
Who brings me to his hut.
Washes my pain. Takes away my anger.

Remember, but do not call my name.
Mother holds me near and I shall never answer again.

Stands-By-Oak - The melded image of the young spirit guide and the older man who lived a solitary life following the death of his family.

An example of spirits existing across time.

Poem 3

The Blue Lady

Palmetto Dunes is one of the oldest developed communities on Hilton Head Island. I remember playing golf on the Arthur Hills course before I knew how to play golf. I must admit I never noticed the lighthouse off the 15th hole. If I ever did see it, I probably thought it was a water tower.

The light sits atop a metal structure. It sits at the end of a dirt path in the middle of a cul-de-sac of private homes. The town, or the PD home owners built a covered space with a picnic bench at the base of the tower.

I need to send someone a thank-you note because the night I decided to try enticing the Blue Lady was one where it would drizzle, then stop. A few minutes later, it would rain, and then stop. This pattern continued to repeat itself, and is well known to people who live here year-round. The tin roof kept me dry, and the table provided a nice spot to sit and strum my guitar.

Before moving on, Stands-By-Oak suggested I try the Irish melodies first when I attempted meeting the ghost of the light. The spirit guide proved correct as a blue shimmering glow emerged from the thin pine woods as I finished the second tune.

I plucked a slow but light pub song and watched the glow become the outline of a body. The body floated towards me, becoming more the image of a young woman as the distance between us diminished.

Seated atop the table, with my feet on the wood meant for seats, I was caught between standing, as a gentleman should, and continuing to play.

Her short brown hair bobbed to the rhythm of the song, so I decided music before manners.

She did wear a blue dress. The night and the reoccurring rain could not obscure the color. In fact, she radiated her own light. This was a new experience for me - relative to ghosts. Taking advantage of the luminescence, I noted a kind oval face beneath the short brown hair. Her hair was damp, but I did not see the rain fall on her. I think this was a permanent look. I could not see color in her eyes, but she had kind eyes. The blue of the dress was royal, and cut in the Victorian manner. A high-neck and a specific waist separating a simple long-sleeved top from a full ankle-length skirt. She was a slender woman.

"My father did not like me listening to such songs," she said. "I played the piano, and always played hymns when he was near enough to hear. I would play other songs when I knew I was alone."

"Thank you for coming," I said. Something about this spirit made me want to be as polite as possible. Not because I feared she might become some raging demon if I treated her poorly. She made me think of times when being courteous was normal.

"Thank you for the songs," she replied.

"Are you Caroline Fripp?"

"My name is Carolina, but I am not related to any Fripps," she answered.

She stood at the end of the table, no further from me than an arm's length.

"It is a story I read," I explained. "You were the daughter of Adam Fripp, the lighthouse keeper. He died during the hurricane of 1898."

Her smile turned to a half-frown for a brief moment - a breath, had either of us been breathing.

"My father was a retired lighthouse keeper," she said. "We lived on a small farm inland and north of here. He would work ten or twelve weeks every year to allow full-time keepers a chance for vacation. The extra money helped, and I often went with him. It was on these trips I heard songs like those you play. My mother died when I was very young, so I either stayed with friends or tagged along."

"I assume you and your father were here when the hurricane came in because the normal keeper was on leave?"

"Both keepers," Carolina said. "Mr. Schwarzer was the Head Keeper. He lived in the cottage where the Front light used to be. That was the white light, and the stairs to the light connected to the house. Mr. Blanding tended the Rear light. This one," she said, her body switched from front to back then she faced me again.

"The Red light," I said.

"Yes." She appeared pleased I knew the color. "The lights were set with the Red higher than the White. From the sound a captain could line them up, Red-atop-White. If he kept his ship in line, he could sail safely through the sand bars. Because I would accompany my father, and I was capable of carrying oil up stairways, both light-keepers were able to leave at the same time."

"Then the hurricane arrived," I prompted.

"We thought it was just a storm at first," she said. "My father realized it was much more after the first few bands of bad weather came through. We hurried to take buckets of oil to the top of both towers. The oil tank was placed outside, so it would be difficult to get more when the strongest winds arrived."

I began to play an Irish lilt. The sound just barely audible. The same technique I used with Gauche when he began retelling his story.

"My father would be responsible for the Rear light. It would be the more difficult to reach and keep lit. I would stay in the front cottage and make sure the oil lamp remained lit. With extra oil already inside, it would be simple for me to keep watch."

She floated around the table, slid by my right as she floated to the other end of the table. She was looking at nothing, but I knew she was watching the Atlantic Ocean churning as water was pushed against the beach and over the dunes.

I did a butt-pivot to follow her. The tune continued.

"It was the second night. Father had been gone much longer than normal. Frightened he might have fallen, I ran to the Rear light. At the top of the stairwell I stepped onto the watch platform. I could hear the wind howling above me. I climbed the ladder to the lantern room. One of the eight windows had broken. My father lay in water and glass."

She turned to face me. She had brown eyes. Sad eyes.

"I thought the glass had cut him, but it was worse. His heart was giving out. He clutched his chest. I knelt and pulled him into my arms. He was so white. His skin cold. The last thing he told me was to keep the lights burning. Ships at sea and all the people on those ships relied on us to bring them in safely. He died having heard my agreement, but never heard me tell him how very much I loved him."

"The stories say your heroic efforts kept both lights shining throughout the storm," I said.

"Ruined my dress," she replied. "Wore me to the bone. It was the end of summer. Until this time, the weather was horribly hot and humid. The rain from the storm was so cold I nearly froze to death. The wind would grow and drop and grow again. The worst of it was entering the Rear lighthouse to bring oil and hear the howling from the broken window above. It was like a thousand dying souls screaming."

"The stories also said you died soon after."

"Three weeks," she answered. "Soon by anyone's measure but mine. I was fevered and do not recall very much. People came. I remember they had to carry my father's body down from the tower. I remember hurting physically. I remember hurting every time I realized my father was gone. I died soon, and it took forever. We're buried near our farm. I don't think anyone knows us there any more."

"Carolina, do you like poetry as well as music?"

"Why, yes. In fact for my birthday that same year my father gave me **The Wayfarers** by Josephine Preston Peabody. He bought it on Charleston on the same day he bought me this dress."

I asked her if she would care to provide a verse for others to know her by, watched the tell-tale flicker which now indicated agreement and some gap placed in time that allowed her to compose her poem.

Darkness lashed by a howling wind,
    I found my soul at ease.
My cheeks damp from hard tears and rain.
    Father's heartbeats did cease
But not his passion for the Light.
    Keep it lit. Give him peace.

Twenty-one, with purpose armored
    Against the raging swell.
Summer freezing wet on my dress,
    I climbed, afraid to fail
Bringing oil for lamps to shine --
    Ships flounder under sail.

Broken glass slashed the blue frill
    Of my dress, now a waste.
Cold water, hot wind, shards of palms
    Lay upon me like paste,
Dragging my spirit to the edge
    Of failure I can taste.

Two nights and more days 'til sunrise
    Yellow rays found me wrung;
Body battered, blue dress gone.
    Others might call me young.
I kept my Father's oath to light
    The way for ships, far flung.

With the battle over,
Too tired to seek cover,
I dreamed of my future lover -
One I would never discover.

White Light.
Red Light.
Heaven's Sight.

Poem 4 & 5

Praise Be In Bluffton

My wife, Sarah, and I live in Bluffton, SC. While we do not reside in the picturesque-turned-touristy Olde Town, our home is less than a mile away. The area is rife in Southern history, from early settlements, tribal Native Americans, battles through several wars, and the changing commerce of the region. Olde Town alone boasts the potential for over a dozen ghosts.

The stories are steeped in history and myth, but only one kept making me want to know more. Not a haunting so much as a haunting sound.

Since the tales of spiritual music drifting through the early morning air are not widely written of, and no one has assigned them to a specific church, I thought I might try and join the choir in an attempt to learn more.

I decided Sundays before sunrise offered my best opportunity. With guitar in a soft-case strapped across my back, I rode my bike into the downtown section of Bluffton.

The first Sunday I sat on the steps of the Church of the Cross on Calhoun Street. The historic, gorgeous Episcopal Church sits beside the May River. I played hymns and simple songs of faith from the 1800s until the sun rose. With no answering voices, I left before early arrivers showed up to prepare for services.

The following Sunday I repeated my ride. I strummed on a bench beside the Bluffton United Methodist Church, just a block away from the Church of the Cross. Besides a cat out hunting a morning snack, I had no visitations.

The Campbell Chapel AME Church on Boundary Street was my third attempt. I should say my third *failed* attempt.

On the fourth excursion I decided to pass on another church. Instead, I rode to the Bluffton Oyster Factory on Wharf Street. The Factory began in 1899, but the locale had been used as a landing for May River boaters for centuries. I thought the history and number of people having come through on their way to or from Savannah (among other places reachable by river) might provide more luck.

Luck did show her friendly side that early morning, but not in the way I expected.

With the sun's first rays on the horizon, I cased my guitar and began my ride back home. As I crossed the bridge on Bridge Street a young man waved and beckoned to me.

"You have the right idea," he said, "but the wrong day."

Avoiding the massive cracks in the roadway where the bridge transitioned back to road, I moved over to the sidewalk. Having done this now for some time, I realized the young black man was an apparition.

"Did the songs call you?" I asked. I know, dumb question, but starting conversations with spirits is never as easy as movies make it appear.

"In a way," he said. "Not my kind of music, but it was nice to hear without all the noise drowning out the rhythms. You're trying to find the singers from the Prayer House. You're playing that kind of music."

"I am, but I'd also like to hear your story."

"Maybe sometime, Brother. The shadows deserve their own recognition."

"Shadows?"

He looked over his shoulder to the eastern skies. Seemed okay with the sun not yet above the pines, and turned back to me.

"Shadows. Echoes. My Mom and Granddad used to tell me about them," he said. "Different types of ghosts. Some are caught in a loop. You can talk with them, but they can't break out of their routine. Some are as free as you and me. We make our own decisions. Some are just echoes from the past. The slaves from the Dubois Prayer House are singing the spirituals from their time."

"You said I had the wrong day."

"Plantation owners made their slaves attend Sunday church with the whites," he said. "They wanted to make damn sure they heard the fire and brimstone awaiting them if they ever slacked off," he hesitated, then added, "or rose up. A Prayer House was built from leftover wood and used by slaves to hold their own services."

"You know a lot about them?"

"My Granddad did," the spirit replied. "He loved history, and he loved teaching it. He told me the Prayer Houses were never very big. Land owners didn't want a large bunch of slaves gathering. They weren't too happy with them meeting at all, but most let the little thrown-together churches alone."

Another glance to the East.

"The inside had no furniture. No pews, no chairs. Wide open so they could sing and dance and give praise to the lord their way. They got together on a weeknight. Since they had to attend *real* church on Sunday. They also worked late, so services began late and often went past midnight. I have to go, but next Wednesday, try playing in the Dubois Park. No shadow will talk with you. Hell, they probably won't even know you're there, but you might get to hear them sing more clearly. Be nice if someone wrote down their spirituals. Having your music written down is having it kept alive."

I could not ask another question, or give him a thank-you. The apparition faded, leaving me with an impression of his smile. I knew this ghost was not an ancient being. For one, his clothes were straight nineteen-sixties or seventies. Loud shirt with a vest, tan slacks with wide cuffs over boots. I once had a similar outfit. I did tell you I was old, didn't I.

Taking the spirit's advice, I drove to Dubois Park the next Wednesday. I closed my health club (Beach City Health and Fitness -- insufferable plug) on Hilton Head Island at 9:00pm. By the time I got home, spent the required minimum amount of time with Sarah and the dogs, it was after 10:00pm.

Dubois Park is one of the truly nice things the Town of Bluffton created. It is a playground for kids, loads of open grassy space for lounging around beneath pines and oaks. There is a common building with restrooms and space for picnics. The Bluffton Historical Preservation Society building is nearby, and the Cottage, the de facto administration building for the park is cute, with a nice covered porch.

Not wanting to draw attention, I set my back against the playground's pirate ship, away from the main road. In the dark, beneath the bow of a huge bending tree, I began to strum old spirituals. True to the word of the Bridge Street ghost, I soon heard the sounds of voices joined together in a happy chorus.

This land must have once housed slave quarters, because the voices were nearby. I could not tell you which direction, or where the original Prayer House might have sit, but the words were easy to understand.

I wish I could provide the melody for you, or explain in words the joy of the choir. I can do neither in this format. I believe the hymn that follows was an original created by someone among the slaves. I have not found it anywhere else.

When the shadows performed it, a strong male voice would lead, answered by full-throated voices. When appropriate, or for the chorus, everyone joined together.

Slave Cabin
https://www.flickr.com/photos/82134796@N03/

Matthew came
                And broke my chains.
Mark held the light
                To guide me home again.

       Luke took away my spirit's pain.
       John washed away my sins.

Don't let darkness fill your heart.
                The sun shall rise tomorrow.
Give unto the Lord His glory.
                He will take away my sorrow.

We must all walk the way
Of the man from Galilee,
Ever striving to be better
Ever better we must be.

We have got to work the plan
Of the Lord who sits above.
We must toil in his employ,
We must teach his perfect love.

Matthew came
                And broke my chains.
Mark held the light
                To guide me home again.

       Luke took away my spirit's pain.

And John

                           Oh Brother John

And John

                           Oh Brother John

         John washed away my sins.

We must all walk the way
Of the man from Galilee,
Ever striving to be better
Ever better we must be.

We have got to work the plan
Of the Lord who sits above.
We must toil in his employ,
We must teach his perfect love.

As the voices broke into the chorus once more, the apparition from Sunday settled on the grass beside me. I started to say something, but he hushed me.

"You seem to have made them happy, Brother," he said. "I think you're about to receive a present."

The present turned out to be a second song. Not another hymn, but a work song used to help pass the time laboring in the heat and humidity of a Lowcountry day.

Consider for a moment the back-breaking work required of these people. Remember they worked regardless of heat, cold, or poor weather. The joy in their voices as this next song came out of the night was an incredible testament to their strength of spirit.

A strong bass voice started the call-and-response format for the work song.

Bend down low

      And pick a little cotton.

Stand back up

      Take another step down.

Bend down low

      And pick a little cotton.

Stand back up

      Take another step down.

Gotta another field waiting

      Gotta pick the whole crop.

Gotta pick this cotton

      'Til the Boss calls stop.

Bend down over

      Lift a heavy bail.

Stand back up

      And throw it in the wagon.

Bend down over

      Lift a heavy bail.

Stand back up

      Toss it next to the other.

Gotta fill this wagon

      Gotta fill it to the top.

Gotta toss these bails

      'Til the Boss calls stop.

I work six days
                Out of every seven.
I work six days
                Just to make it to Heaven.

Gots three more days
                Gotta work my best.
Gots three more days
                'Til Sunday when I rest.

I cannot tell you for certain the young black man was Tony Hooks. I do know his mother, Sarah Riley Hooks lived on Bridge Street. I know his grandfather was Michael C. Riley, one of the most influential African-Americans in Beaufort County during the time of the Civil Rights movements. He was considered responsible for making sure young black children received quality educations. The elementary school in Bluffton is named for him: M.C. Riley Elementary School on Burnt Church Road.

Tony was a talented guitarist who played with Sly and the Family Stone and with another Bluffton legend, musician, and songwriter, John Brennan. Tony was shot, murdered on his mother's porch. I have yet to discover why.

I hope one day to meet him again. I'd love to hear his story from his perspective, and, perhaps, a poem.

Poem 6

Forlorn

If you are thinking I do pretty well with finding and conversing with the dead, let me dissuade you of that opinion. The active encounters to this point took over a calendar year to accomplish. I have many more failures than successes.

Not every failure resulted in time spent alone playing music from eras long past.

Among my more successful failures was seeing a phantom wagon-hearse pulled by four large black horses. This sighting occurred in Sea Pines Plantation near the old Stoney-Baynard Plantation ruins. I thought this an example of an echo from the past, until the driver looked directly at me. His scowl did not fill me with confidence to approach nearer. The whip in his hands was, most likely, as unsubstantial as the spirit at the reins of the team. I did not test the theory.

I walked the beach on St. Helena Island, but never found more than starfish and a few sharks' teeth. Do not belittle my discoveries. Finding sharks' teeth on a beach in the dark is no small feat. The beach is very nice, and the island is one of several around Beaufort worth visiting. I caution you to best keep your visits to daylight. Bad things can happen on lonely stretches of coastline after dark, and not always caused by those who have passed beyond.

The famous haunted Chapel of Ease on St. Helena's Island did have echoes wandering about. The forms too fuzzy for me to determine anything as to gender or period. They made no sign my presence made any difference to their travels around the old cemetery, crypt, or ruins.

I read the story of the Chapel's crypt, plundered by Union soldiers during the Civil War, then caught in a huge forest fire in the 1900s. Workers were hired to rebuild the entrance, only to find their bricks removed and stacked to the side each morning on their return. The bricks are no longer there, stacked or otherwise. The crypt's entrance was not repaired. One for the ghosts.

The Fripp Island Lighthouse provided none of the grist I got from the Leamington Lighthouse on Hilton Head.

Not wanting to venture into the too-often told hauntings of Charleston, to the North or Savannah, to the South, the furtherest I went for a story was the small town of Yamassee. Named for Stands-By-Oak's people.

The small town is located just off Interstate Highway 95, and for a small town, it holds as much history as the cities of Charleston, Beaufort, or Savannah. The one most significant part of its history is the Old Sheldon Church. Built between 1745 and 1755, it is the first Anglican church built in North America based on a temple design.

The ruins are easy to find [there is a road named Old Sheldon Church Road] The chapel walls and columns, as well as they adjoining cemetery, sit on private property. The site is managed by St. Helena's Church in Beaufort, SC. I say this because you must take care if you visit the ruins. There are rules.

The church was burned during the Revolutionary War, rebuilt, and burned again by Sherman's troops at the end of the Civil War. It was not rebuilt following the second fire.

During the day, it is a beautiful location. People even use it for weddings. At night, shadowed by moss-covered live oaks and surrounded by sarcophagi and grave markers (ancient and relatively new), it is one of the spookiest places on Earth.

The only odd thing about this old church being haunted is stories are told of only one ghost in residence. Considering the history, the number of burials, and the people who must have attended services since the first one in 1757, I would be more likely to believe a host of spirits remained attached to the ruins.

A woman, dressed in what is described only as dressed as a Pilgrim, appears to people, usually at dusk, and usually near the grave of an infant. There are several graves marked with the names of young boys and girls who died too soon, and others with the epitaph *Infant Child Of*. None I saw fit the time period for someone dressed as a Pilgrim.

Curiosity fully in command, I set my back against a marble box which once held a famous man's remains. I pulled my guitar from the soft case, placed my backpack with light, water, paper, pen, and snacks on top of the case, and set up shop. I already snapped several photographs with my I-phone. The phone always accompanied me, but not once did I attempt to photograph any of the specters from previous encounters. The thought of asking for a selfie while trying to entice poetry from a spook simply never crossed my mind.

A little musical history research left me overwhelmed with the number of potential styles I might use to bait the ghost lady. The wide-ranging ethnic diversity immigrating from Europe to the Colonies brought their music with them. Considering the Sheldon Church was named for Sheldon, England, the ancestral home of William Bull, the local plantation owner who paid to build it, and that it was an Anglican place of worship, I decided on English ballads of the period.

As it was nearing sundown when I began, a couple of couples still wandered the ruins and graveyard. Both pair, separately, stopped to listen. They were kind enough to pretend to enjoy my playing. By the time the sun set, and the shadows morphed into shades of dark and darker, I played without an audience.

I only learned four ballads, and my third rendition of the one called *Legend of Willie Williams* proved to be the charm.

Standing beside another marble sarcophagus, the shape of a woman in a long dress. I must have dropped my eyes (I cheat and look at my fingering more often than I should.), because I looked up and she stood there.

"Please stop," she said. Not angry. Her voice did not strike me as anything but strong and sad.

"I didn't mean to offend you," I said, my right hand resting atop the body of the instrument.

"You did not," she answered. "The song made me happy, and I have no cause to ever be happy. It reminded me of home. I will never see home again."

She moved closer. I could not tell, in the lack of light, if she was pretty, plain, or ugly. Her face obscured by darkness -- by choice? She did wear a brown dress. The landscape lights used as security for the ruins produced enough lambent light to discern the milk-chocolate hue. I saw now why she was described as a Pilgrim. A frilled, high shift covered her neck, and she wore a light-brown waistcoat closed with buttons. She had on a petticoat dress of the same color. This is why it appeared she wore a single dress, not a two-piece outfit. An apron spread across the front of the dress. Instead of the white I imagine when I picture Pilgrim housewives, this one dyed a darker shade of chocolate.

I tried to make out features as she hovered within a few feet of me. All I can say is she did not wear a coif, and her hair hung straight and loose to her shoulders.

"This isn't your home?"

"I came from Wales," the sadness choking down the strength of her voice. "I followed the love of me life, William. He came here as an indentured servant. He had such a wonderful way with animals. Horses especially. He sent back a letter. He wrote of how beautiful this new land was, and how he worked in the stables of a plantation so large he had not yet seen all of it."

"Can I know your name?"

"Ruth," she answered. Nothing more. "My family and his were Quakers. Being Welsh and being a Quaker was difficult. It is why William accepted the seven-years of service. To escape the hatred, and, after his service, open a blacksmith trade. He would send for me when he could. He promised. But I could not wait."

The ghost of Ruth turned away, walking back toward the graveyard. I set my guitar aside and followed. Rewarded when she continued her story.

"I went to the man who arranged for people to work in the colonies. I was thrilled when he said he could place me as an indentured maid in the same plantation as William. I accepted, signed my name, did not tell my parents or my sister. I slipped away on the night before the ship sailed from Aberdaron."

She stopped between two standing grave markers. "I was raped by a sailor before we reached Charleston. He swore he would kill me if I told anyone. By the time I reached the Plantation and found William, I was pregnant. Beginning to show."

The apparition moved ahead a few feet and stopped once more.

"He would have nothing to do with me." The mournful tone almost crushed my own heart. I am not the most empathetic person, but I felt tears forming. "That it was not by my choice did not matter to him. His love was not strong enough to bare a wife with a child by another man."

Ghosts, as you may or may not realize, do not breath. Ruth produced a sigh of resignation that emptied her soul from her form when she released it.

"I worked as a maid in the Master's sister's house. It was far away from the main stables, so I never saw William. Five months later my little girl died the same day of her birth. I carried her here. The church was under construction, but only the outer walls stood. It would one day be consecrated ground, and she deserved that. I dug her grave with my own hands, placed her, wrapped in a white apron, within, and covered her over. No one could tell a small grave existed within the holdings."

A glimmer of soft yellow spread across a small section of ground. It existed only a moment. I recognized the spot as near one of the infant gravestones.

"I came every day to say a prayer for Rebecca. I forgave William, but I never loved again. One week before the end of my servitude I came down with a fever. I knew I would die. I wanted so badly to be buried next to Rebecca, but I could not tell anyone. If they knew, she would have been removed."

She turned and looked at me across her shoulder. I can tell you now Ruth was a beautiful woman with eyes old and lips permanently locked into a frown.

"They completed the church before I died. It was the most glorious temple I had ever seen. The church, the trees, the place where Rebecca would rest forever could not have been more perfect. I don't know where they buried my body. I imagine in an unmarked grave for the poor whites. It did not matter. It does not matter. I can visit my child and say a prayer for her every day."

Ruth spoke to me, but she looked away, speaking to the world at the same time.

"Quakers do not believe in heaven and hell," she said. "How you live your life is the most important thing you do for God. But when you do not have a chance at life, I am not certain what God may think. I hope my prayers fill in for the goodness she might have done."

"Would you compose a poem for me?" I asked. "If others know of Ruth and Rebecca, maybe they will add their prayers to yours."

A flicker of her ghostly form, the browns fading then returning, followed by the voice bolstered by the strength of her love.

OLD SHELDON CHURCH RUINS
ATTRIBUTION: LJB06

Rebecca lives within my heart.
Her eyes never saw me.
Her fingers never closed on mine.
But we will never be apart.

Rebecca lives within my soul.
No one knew her name.
No one saw her smile.
Her story goes untold.

Rebecca lives in my memory.
I keep her evermore
As my spirit walks this place.
My duty for eternity.

Rebecca lives now with you
And she will bring you peace.
Her life will have had meaning -
While yours will be renewed.

I apologize if any of the poems are lacking in some literary way. I tried to remember them, writing them down as quickly as I could, but I am sure I made mistakes. Those mistakes are to be attributed to me, not the spirits.

If you enjoyed the stories, histories, and poetry of the haunted Lowcountry of South Carolina, please consider leaving a short review at Amazon.com. Such reviews make it possible for others to find books like PARANORMAL POETRY.

Other books, fiction and poetry, can be sampled at donfoxe.com. Feel free to use the CONTACT page to join my newsletter, or simply leave a message. It's all good.

Sincerely,

Don

www.ingramcontent.com/pod-product-compliance
Lightning Source LLC
LaVergne TN
LVHW010023070426

835508LV00001B/26